WEEKLY WR READER

EARLY LEARNING LIBRARY

My Day at School/
Mi día en la escuela

After School/
Después de la escuela

by/por Joanne Mattern

Reading consultant/Consultora de lectura:
Susan Nations, M.Ed.,
author, literacy coach,
consultant in literacy development/
autora, tutora de alfabetización,
consultora de desarrollo de la lectura

Please visit our web site at: www.garethstevens.com
For a free color catalog describing Weekly Reader® Early Learning Library's list
of high-quality books, call 1-877-445-5824 (USA) or 1-800-387-3178 (Canada).
Weekly Reader® Early Learning Library's fax: (414) 336-0164.

Library of Congress Cataloging-in-Publication Data

Mattern, Joanne, 1963-
    [After school. Spanish & English]
    After school = Después de la escuela / by/por Joanne Mattern.
       p. cm. — (My day at school = Mi día en la escuela)
    Includes bibliographical references and index.
    ISBN-10: 0-8368-7357-2 — ISBN-13: 978-0-8368-7357-3 (lib. bdg.)
    ISBN-10: 0-8368-7364-5 — ISBN-13: 978-0-8368-7364-1 (softcover)
    1. School children—Juvenile literature. I. Title. II. Title: Después de la escuela.
  III. Series: Mattern, Joanne, 1963- My day at school.
  HQ781.M36218   2007
  372.18—dc22   2006017289

This edition first published in 2007 by
Weekly Reader® Early Learning Library
A Member of the WRC Media Family of Companies
330 West Olive Street, Suite 100
Milwaukee, WI 53212 USA

Editor: Barbara Kiely Miller
Art direction: Tammy West
Cover design and page layout: Kami Strunsee
Picture research: Diane Laska-Swanke
Photographer: Gregg Andersen
Translators: Tatiana Acosta and Guillermo Gutiérrez

Printed in the United States of America

1 2 3 4 5 6 7 8 9 10 09 08 07 06

Note to Educators and Parents

Reading is such an exciting adventure for young children! They are beginning to integrate their oral language skills with written language. To encourage children along the path to early literacy, books must be colorful, engaging, and interesting; they should invite the young reader to explore both the print and the pictures.

The *My Day at School* series is designed to help young readers review the routines and rules of a school day, while learning new vocabulary and strengthening their reading comprehension. In simple, easy-to-read language, each book follows a child through part of a typical school day.

Each book is specially designed to support the young reader in the reading process. The familiar topics are appealing to young children and invite them to read — and re-read — again and again. The full-color photographs and enhanced text further support the student during the reading process.

In addition to serving as wonderful picture books in schools, libraries, homes, and other places where children learn to love reading, these books are specifically intended to be read within an instructional guided reading group. This small group setting allows beginning readers to work with a fluent adult model as they make meaning from the text. After children develop fluency with the text and content, the book can be read independently. Children and adults alike will find these books supportive, engaging, and fun!

— Susan Nations, M.Ed., author, literacy coach,
and consultant in literacy development

Nota para los maestros y los padres

¡Leer es una aventura tan emocionante para los niños pequeños! A esta edad están comenzando a integrar su manejo del lenguaje oral con el lenguaje escrito. Para animar a los niños en el camino de la lectura incipiente, los libros deben ser coloridos, estimulantes e interesantes; deben invitar a los jóvenes lectores a explorar la letra impresa y las ilustraciones.

La serie *Mi día en la escuela* está pensada para ayudar a los jóvenes lectores a repasar las actividades y normas de un día de escuela, mientras enriquecen su vocabulario y refuerzan su comprensión. Cada libro presenta, en un lenguaje sencillo y fácil de entender, las actividades de un niño durante parte de un típico día escolar.

Cada libro está especialmente diseñado para ayudar al joven lector en el proceso de lectura. Los temas familiares llaman la atención de los niños y los invitan a leer —y releer— una y otra vez. Las fotografías a todo color y el tamaño de la letra ayudan aún más al estudiante en el proceso de lectura.

Además de servir como maravillosos libros ilustrados en escuelas, bibliotecas, hogares y otros lugares donde los niños aprenden a amar la lectura, estos libros han sido especialmente concebidos para ser leídos en un grupo de lectura guiada. Este contexto permite que los lectores incipientes trabajen con un adulto que domina la lectura mientras van determinando el significado del texto. Una vez que los niños dominan el texto y el contenido, el libro puede ser leído de manera independiente. ¡Estos libros les resultarán útiles, estimulantes y divertidos a niños y a adultos por igual!

— Susan Nations, M.Ed., autora/tutora de alfabetización/
consultora de desarrollo de la lectura

School is over. It is time

to go home.

- - - - - - - - - - - - -

Terminó la escuela. Es hora de

ir a casa.

I take the **school bus** home.

Mom is waiting for me.

- - - - - - - - - - - - - -

Voy a casa en el **autobús escolar**.

Mamá me está esperando.

SCHOOL BUS

SPEED
LIMIT
20

668-641

7

I put my **backpack** on the table.

I hang up my coat.

- - - - - - - - - - - - - -

Pongo la **mochila** sobre la mesa.

Cuelgo mi chaqueta.

I am hungry. Mom makes

a snack for me.

- - - - - - - - - - - -

Tengo hambre. Mamá me prepara

algo para merendar.

11

Then I play outside. I like

to ride my bike.

Después, salgo fuera a jugar.

Me gusta montar en bicicleta.

Now it is time for my **karate lesson**.

Mom drives me to the class.

— — — — — — — — — — — —

Ha llegado la hora de mi **clase de karate**. Mamá me lleva.

I do my **homework** before dinner.

Mom helps me sometimes.

- - - - - - - - - - - - - -

Antes de cenar hago mis **tareas**.

Mamá me ayuda algunas veces.

I read a book after dinner.

I brought the book home from

school. Dad listens to me read.

- - - - - - - - - - - - -

Después de la cena leo un libro.

Este libro lo traje de la escuela.

Papá me oye leer.

Then I watch TV with Dad. Soon I will go to bed. Tomorrow is a new day at school!

- - - - - - - - - - - -

Después veo la televisión con papá. Pronto me iré a la cama. ¡Mañana será otro día de escuela!

Glossary

backpack — a bag worn on the back to carry books and supplies

homework — school work that is done at home

hungry — wanting food to eat

karate — a form of self-defense that uses kicks and punches

lesson — a class or happening that teaches something

school bus — a bus that students take to and from school

Glosario

autobús escolar — autobús que los estudiantes toman para ir a la escuela y volver a casa

clase — lección o enseñanza que nos ayuda a aprender algo

hambre — ganas de comer

karate — forma de defensa personal que usa patadas y puñetazos

mochila — bolsa que se lleva en la espalda para cargar libros y material

tareas — trabajo escolar que se hace en casa

For More Information/Más información

Books

After School Stuff. Cara J. Stevens (Lowell House Juvenile)

Bike Riding. After-School Fun (series). JoAnn Early Macken
(Gareth Stevens)

Karate. After-School Fun (series). JoAnn Early Macken
(Gareth Stevens)

Libros

Bicicletas. Ruedas, alas y agua (series). Lola M. Schaefer
(Heinemann)

El chico karateka. Ann Morris (Penguin)

Index

Índice

About the Author

Joanne Mattern has written more than one hundred and fifty books for children. Joanne also works in her local library. She lives in New York State with her husband, three daughters, and assorted pets. She enjoys animals, music, going to baseball games, reading, and visiting schools to talk about her books.

Información sobre la autora

Joanne Mattern ha escrito más de ciento cincuenta libros para niños. Además, Joanne trabaja en la biblioteca de su comunidad. Vive en el estado de Nueva York con su esposo, sus tres hijas y varias mascotas. A Joanne le gustan los animales, la música, ir al béisbol, leer y hacer visitas a las escuelas para hablar de sus libros.